THE MILLIONAIRE
MINDSET BLUEPRINT

Unleash Your Potential and Build Wealth

Patrick Kay

Kay Press

ISBN: 9798851647796

Cover design by: Kay Press

Preface

Welcome to *"The Millionaire Mindset Blueprint: Unleash Your Potential and Build Wealth."* This book is your guide to unlocking the hidden potential within you and transforming your financial destiny. It is an invitation to explore the transformative power of a millionaire mindset and to embark on a journey towards financial abundance and freedom.

In these pages, we will delve into the core principles, strategies, and mindset shifts that are fundamental to achieving extraordinary financial success. We will challenge conventional beliefs about wealth and unveil the blueprint that has guided countless individuals on their path to riches. Prepare to discover the untapped reservoirs of potential that lie within you and to harness them for the creation of wealth and prosperity.

This book is not just about accumulating material riches; it is about embracing a mindset that propels you towards holistic success. It is about aligning your thoughts, beliefs, and actions with the vision of a life filled with abundance, purpose, and fulfillment. The millionaire mindset is not limited to financial wealth alone; it encompasses a profound shift in how you perceive yourself, your capabilities, and the possibilities that surround you.

Throughout this journey, we will explore the psychological, emotional, and behavioral aspects that shape our relationship with money. We will uncover the limiting beliefs, fears, and self-imposed barriers that often prevent us from attaining the financial success we desire. By understanding and reshaping our mindset, we can pave the way for extraordinary abundance and unlock our full potential.

The chapters that follow will guide you through a systematic process of transformation. We will explore the power of intention, visualization, and goal setting to create a clear path towards wealth creation. We will delve into the art of strategic planning, risk management, and leveraging opportunities for exponential growth.

We will also explore the significance of multiple streams of income, smart money management, and the principles of effective investing. You will learn how to leverage your skills, talents, and passions to build profitable ventures and create lasting financial abundance. We will equip you with the tools and strategies needed to navigate the ever-changing landscape of entrepreneurship and seize the right opportunities at the right time.

But building wealth is not just about amassing riches for personal gain. It is about using your resources to make a positive impact on the world around you. We will explore the power of giving back, philanthropy, and creating a legacy that extends far beyond financial success. Through conscious and responsible wealth creation, you can contribute to the betterment of society and leave a lasting imprint on future generations.

As you embark on this journey, I encourage you to approach each chapter with an open mind and a willingness to challenge your existing beliefs and behaviors. The exercises, reflections, and practical tools provided throughout the book will empower you to take immediate action and integrate the millionaire mindset into your daily life.

Remember, the path to wealth and abundance is not a destination but a lifelong journey of growth and expansion. It requires commitment, resilience, and a relentless pursuit of personal and financial excellence. As you progress through this book, embrace every opportunity to learn, evolve, and transcend your current limitations.

The Millionaire Mindset Blueprint is your roadmap to unleash your full potential and build the wealth you desire. It is time to release the shackles of self-doubt and step into the realm of unlimited possibilities. Together, let us embark on this extraordinary adventure and create a life of abundance, impact, and fulfillment.

Get ready to unleash your potential and unlock the doors to financial freedom. Your journey to building wealth starts now.

Contents

Title Page

Copyright

Preface

Chapter 1: The Psychology of Wealth: Understanding Your Relationship with Money   3

Chapter 2: Cultivating a Wealth Mindset: Overcoming Limiting Beliefs and Embracing Abundance   6

Chapter 3: Rewiring Your Subconscious: Programming Your Mind for Success   9

Chapter 4: Goal Setting and Visualization: Manifesting Your Financial Dreams   12

Chapter 5: Multiple Streams of Income: Creating Wealth-Building Channels   17

Chapter 6: Smart Money Management: Budgeting, Saving, and Debt Reduction   20

Chapter 7: The Art of Investing: Building and Diversifying Your Portfolio   23

Chapter 8: Entrepreneurship and Wealth Creation: From Ideas to Profitable Ventures   26

Chapter 9: Resilience and Persistence: Overcoming Obstacles on Your Path to Wealth   31

Chapter 10: Embracing Risk: Calculated Moves for Financial Growth   34

Chapter 11: Learning from Failure: Transforming Setbacks into Opportunities   37

Chapter 12: Building a Support Network: Surrounding   40
Yourself with Like-Minded Individuals

Chapter 13: Identifying Lucrative Trends and Markets: The   45
Power of Research and Analysis

Chapter 14: Seizing Opportunities: Timing, Preparation, and   48
Action

Chapter 15: Networking and Strategic Relationships: 51
Opening Doors to Success

Chapter 16: Innovation and Adaptability: Thriving in a   54
Dynamic Financial Landscape

Chapter 17: Financial Freedom and Lifestyle Design: 59
Creating the Life You Desire

Chapter 18: Giving Back and Impact: Using Wealth to Make a   62
Difference

Chapter 19: Legacy Building: Leaving a Lasting Financial and   65
Emotional Heritage

Chapter 20: The Journey Continues: Sustaining Your   68
Millionaire Mindset

Conclusion: Your Path to Financial Greatness   71

Appendix: Resources and Tools for Continued Growth   73

Disclaimer   76

Part I: Shifting Your Mindset

Chapter 1: The Psychology of Wealth: Understanding Your Relationship with Money

Introduction:

In this opening chapter, we delve into the fascinating realm of the psychology of wealth. We explore the intricate dynamics that shape our relationship with money and how our thoughts, beliefs, and emotions influence our financial decisions and outcomes. By gaining a deeper understanding of our psychological relationship with money, we can begin to transform our mindset and set the stage for financial success.

1.1 The Money Mindset:

We begin by exploring the concept of the money mindset and its profound impact on our financial reality. Uncover the subconscious beliefs and attitudes that have been ingrained within us since childhood and shape our financial behaviors. Learn to identify and challenge any negative or limiting beliefs about money, abundance, and wealth, allowing for the development of a positive and empowered money mindset.

1.2 Your Money Story:

Every individual has a unique money story—a narrative that has shaped their perception and behavior around money. Dive into your own money story and reflect upon the experiences, messages, and influences that have shaped your relationship with money. By understanding the origins of your beliefs and behaviors, you can consciously choose to rewrite your money story and create a healthier and more empowering narrative.

1.3 Emotional Factors in Financial Decision-Making:

Emotions play a significant role in our financial decisions and behaviors. Explore the various emotions, such as fear, greed, guilt, and shame, that often influence our relationship with money. Discover strategies for managing and navigating these emotions effectively, allowing for more rational and intentional financial decision-making. By cultivating emotional intelligence and awareness, we can make wiser choices that align with our long-term financial goals.

1.4 The Influence of Money Scripts:

Money scripts are the unconscious beliefs and scripts we carry about money that impact our financial behaviors. Uncover your own money scripts and explore how they shape your financial habits and patterns. Evaluate whether these scripts serve you or hinder your financial progress. Through self-reflection and conscious rewriting of your money scripts, you can reshape your beliefs and develop healthier and more empowering money narratives.

1.5 The Impact of Money Mindset on Wealth Creation:

Understand the crucial connection between mindset and wealth creation. Explore the ways in which a positive money mindset can attract opportunities, increase financial resilience, and foster a growth-oriented approach to wealth creation. Discover practical strategies for shifting your money mindset, including affirmations, visualization, and gratitude practices, to align your thoughts and beliefs with your financial aspirations.

1.6 Overcoming Psychological Barriers to Wealth:

Many individuals face psychological barriers that hinder their path to financial success. Explore common barriers, such as fear of failure, imposter syndrome, and self-sabotage, that can hold us back from achieving our full potential. Learn strategies and techniques to overcome these psychological barriers, cultivate self-confidence, and develop a resilient mindset that empowers you to take bold actions towards financial greatness.

Conclusion:

As we conclude this first chapter, you have gained a deeper understanding of the psychology of wealth and the profound influence it has on your financial journey. By becoming aware of your money mindset, exploring your money story, and addressing psychological barriers, you have taken the first steps towards transforming your relationship with money. In the chapters to come, we will explore practical strategies and insights that will further empower you to develop a healthy mindset and build a solid foundation for achieving lasting financial success. Get ready to unlock your potential and embrace a new mindset that paves the way for abundant wealth and fulfillment.

Chapter 2: Cultivating a Wealth Mindset: Overcoming Limiting Beliefs and Embracing Abundance

Introduction:

In this chapter, we delve deeper into the process of cultivating a wealth mindset—an essential component of achieving financial success. We explore the power of our thoughts, beliefs, and perceptions in shaping our financial reality. By identifying and overcoming limiting beliefs and embracing abundance, we can unlock our true potential and attract wealth into our lives.

2.1 Unmasking Limiting Beliefs:

We begin by uncovering the limiting beliefs that may be holding us back from experiencing financial abundance. Explore the common negative beliefs around money, success, and wealth that often hinder our progress. Through introspection and reflection, identify the specific limiting beliefs that have influenced your financial behaviors and outcomes. By bringing them into the light, you can challenge and replace them with empowering beliefs that support your financial goals.

2.2 The Power of Positive Affirmations:

Positive affirmations are transformative tools that can rewire your subconscious mind and shift your mindset towards abundance and wealth. Discover the power of affirmations and how to create personalized statements that align with your financial aspirations. Learn practical techniques for incorporating affirmations into your daily routine, reinforcing positive beliefs, and attracting opportunities for financial growth.

2.3 Embracing a Wealth Mindset:

Shift your mindset from scarcity to abundance. Explore the mindset traits and habits of successful individuals who have achieved financial greatness. Cultivate a wealth mindset by embracing gratitude, optimism, and a focus on possibilities. Develop a mindset that sees opportunities instead of obstacles, and views failures as valuable learning experiences. Discover practical strategies for adopting a wealth mindset and integrating it into all aspects of your life.

2.4 Rewriting Your Financial Story:

Our financial story is the narrative we have created around our past and current financial experiences. Dive into your own financial story and evaluate how it has shaped your beliefs and behaviors. Discover techniques for reframing negative experiences, releasing financial regrets, and rewriting a new and empowering financial story. By changing the narrative, you can create a fresh perspective and open yourself to new possibilities.

2.5 Visualization and Manifestation Techniques:

Harness the power of visualization and manifestation to create the financial reality you desire. Explore visualization techniques that allow you to vividly imagine and experience your desired financial outcomes. Learn how to align your thoughts, emotions, and actions with your financial goals through intentional visualization practices. Discover how manifestation techniques can help you attract the resources, opportunities, and wealth needed to achieve your dreams.

2.6 Surrounding Yourself with Abundance:

The people and environments we surround ourselves with significantly impact our mindset and beliefs. Explore the importance of surrounding yourself with individuals who embody abundance and success. Learn to create a supportive network of like-minded individuals who inspire and uplift you on your financial journey. Discover techniques for curating an environment that nurtures your wealth mindset and reinforces your beliefs in abundance.

Conclusion:

As we conclude this chapter, you have gained a deeper understanding of the wealth mindset and its transformative power in achieving financial success. By identifying and overcoming limiting beliefs, embracing abundance, and rewiring your financial story, you have taken significant steps towards cultivating a mindset that attracts wealth and prosperity. In the chapters to come, we will explore practical strategies and insights that will further empower you to strengthen your wealth mindset and align your thoughts, beliefs, and actions with your financial goals. Get ready to step into a mindset of abundance and unleash your full potential for financial greatness.

Chapter 3: Rewiring Your Subconscious: Programming Your Mind for Success

Introduction:

In this chapter, we delve into the power of your subconscious mind and its influence on your financial success. We explore techniques and strategies for rewiring your subconscious programming to align with your goals and aspirations. By harnessing the power of your subconscious, you can overcome self-sabotaging patterns and create a solid foundation for long-term success.

3.1 Understanding the Subconscious Mind:

We begin by delving into the workings of your subconscious mind. Explore the difference between the conscious and subconscious aspects of your mind and their respective roles in shaping your thoughts, beliefs, and behaviors. Gain insights into the depth of your subconscious programming and how it influences your financial decisions and outcomes.

3.2 The Power of Repetition and Reinforcement:

Discover the importance of repetition and reinforcement in reprogramming your subconscious mind. Explore techniques such as affirmations, visualizations, and positive self-talk that can create new neural pathways and overwrite old, limiting beliefs. Learn how consistent and focused repetition can gradually replace negative thought patterns with positive and empowering ones.

3.3 Affirmations and Auto-Suggestion:

Deep dive into the transformative power of affirmations and auto-suggestion. Explore techniques for creating effective affirmations that resonate with your subconscious mind. Understand the mechanics of how affirmations work and how to integrate them into your daily routine for maximum impact. Learn how to overcome resistance and skepticism to fully harness the power of affirmations in rewiring your subconscious.

3.4 Hypnosis and Subliminal Programming:

Explore the use of hypnosis and subliminal programming as tools for reprogramming the subconscious mind. Understand how hypnosis can bypass the critical conscious mind and create lasting positive changes at the subconscious level. Learn about subliminal messaging and how it can be used to implant empowering beliefs and suggestions in your subconscious mind.

3.5 Visualization and Imagination Techniques:

Harness the power of visualization and imagination to activate your subconscious mind. Learn how to vividly imagine and visualize your financial success, programming your subconscious with powerful mental images. Explore techniques for enhancing your visualization practice, including sensory engagement, emotional involvement, and incorporating details that make your visualizations more vivid and compelling.

3.6 Mindfulness and Self-Awareness:

Develop mindfulness and self-awareness as essential tools for rewiring your subconscious mind. Explore techniques for cultivating present-moment awareness and observing your thoughts and beliefs without judgment. Through mindfulness practices, gain clarity on your subconscious programming and identify any patterns or beliefs that are not aligned with your financial goals. By cultivating self-awareness, you can consciously choose to shift and reprogram your subconscious mind.

Conclusion:

As we conclude this chapter, you have gained valuable insights into the power of rewiring your subconscious mind for success. By understanding the workings of your subconscious, harnessing the repetition and reinforcement of positive programming, and exploring techniques such as affirmations, hypnosis, visualization, and mindfulness, you have the tools to reprogram your subconscious mind in alignment with your financial goals. In the chapters ahead, we will further explore practical strategies and insights that will empower you to continue rewiring your subconscious and create a solid foundation for sustained financial success. Get ready to tap into the immense power of your subconscious mind and pave the way for the manifestation of your financial dreams.

Chapter 4: Goal Setting and Visualization: Manifesting Your Financial Dreams

Introduction:

In this chapter, we explore the powerful synergy between goal setting and visualization as essential tools for manifesting your financial dreams. We delve into the art of setting clear, inspiring goals and leveraging the creative power of visualization to bring those goals to life. By aligning your thoughts, intentions, and actions, you can harness the law of attraction and manifest your desired financial reality.

4.1 The Art of Goal Setting:

We begin by understanding the art of goal setting and its transformative impact on your financial journey. Learn the key principles of effective goal setting, including specificity, measurability, achievability, relevance, and time-bound nature. Explore the different types of goals, such as short-term, medium-term, and long-term, and the importance of setting goals that align with your values and aspirations.

4.2 Creating a Compelling Vision:

Develop a compelling vision that serves as the driving force behind your financial goals. Explore techniques for clarifying your vision and gaining a crystal-clear picture of your desired financial reality. Dive into the details of what your life looks like when you have achieved your financial dreams, including your lifestyle, relationships, contributions, and overall fulfillment.

4.3 Visualization Techniques for Goal Manifestation:

Harness the power of visualization to manifest your financial dreams. Explore visualization techniques that enable you to vividly imagine and experience your goals as already accomplished. Learn how to engage all your senses in the visualization process, making it more immersive and impactful. Practice visualization regularly to align your subconscious mind with your financial goals and attract the resources, opportunities, and experiences necessary for their realization.

4.4 Creating Vision Boards:

Discover the creative process of creating vision boards as tangible representations of your financial dreams. Learn how to collect and arrange images, words, and symbols that resonate with your goals and aspirations. Explore different ways to create vision boards, including physical collages or digital versions. By regularly observing your vision board, you reinforce your goals and immerse yourself in the energy of their manifestation.

4.5 Affirmations for Goal Alignment:

Integrate affirmations into your goal-setting and visualization practice. Explore how affirmations can align your thoughts, beliefs, and actions with your financial goals. Create personalized affirmations that affirm your abilities, worthiness, and alignment with your desired financial outcomes. Learn techniques for incorporating affirmations into your daily routine and maximizing their effectiveness in supporting your visualization practice.

4.6 Reviewing, Adjusting, and Celebrating Your Progress:

Regularly review and adjust your goals and visualization practices to stay aligned with your evolving aspirations. Learn how to evaluate your progress, celebrate milestones, and make any necessary course corrections along the way. Celebrate your achievements and acknowledge the progress you have made, reinforcing positive habits and inspiring continued momentum towards your financial dreams.

Conclusion:

As we conclude this chapter, you have gained a deep understanding of the symbiotic relationship between goal setting and visualization in manifesting your financial dreams. By setting clear, inspiring goals and leveraging the power of visualization, you tap into the creative forces of the universe and align your thoughts, intentions, and actions towards your desired financial reality. In the chapters ahead, we will explore practical strategies and insights that will empower you to further enhance your goal setting and visualization practices, fueling the manifestation of your financial dreams. Get ready to immerse yourself in the transformative power of goal setting and visualization, as you embark on a journey of abundant financial manifestation.

Part II: Strategies for Financial Success

Chapter 5: Multiple Streams of Income: Creating Wealth-Building Channels

Introduction:

In Part 2 of this book, we shift our focus to practical strategies for creating multiple streams of income—an essential pillar of building sustainable wealth. In this chapter, we explore the concept of multiple income streams and the benefits they bring to your financial journey. By diversifying your income sources, you can enhance your financial security, unlock new opportunities, and accelerate your path to financial greatness.

5.1 Understanding Multiple Streams of Income:

We begin by understanding the concept of multiple streams of income and why it is crucial for long-term financial success. Explore the different types of income streams, such as active income, passive income, and portfolio income. Gain insights into the advantages of having multiple income streams, including increased financial stability, flexibility, and the ability to generate wealth even during economic uncertainties.

5.2 Assessing Your Skills, Talents, and Passions:

Discover your unique skills, talents, and passions that can serve as the foundation for creating multiple income streams. Assess your areas of expertise and interests to identify potential income-generating opportunities. Explore ways to leverage your strengths and align them with market demands, ensuring that your income streams align with your personal values and aspirations.

5.3 Active Income Streams:

Explore various active income streams that can generate immediate cash flow. Learn about traditional employment, freelancing, consulting, and entrepreneurship as avenues for active income. Discover strategies for optimizing your earning potential in these areas and how to leverage your skills and expertise to create valuable products or services.

5.4 Passive Income Streams:

Dive into the world of passive income and explore strategies for generating income with minimal ongoing effort. Learn about real estate investments, dividend-paying stocks, peer-to-peer lending, and online businesses as potential sources of passive income. Understand the importance of initial investment and setting up systems that generate income even when you are not actively involved.

5.5 Creating a Portfolio of Income Streams:

Discover the power of building a diversified portfolio of income streams. Explore the benefits of combining active, passive, and portfolio income streams to maximize your financial potential. Learn techniques for assessing the risk and return profiles of different income streams and optimizing your portfolio to achieve a balance between stability and growth.

5.6 Exploring New Opportunities and Emerging Trends:

Stay abreast of new opportunities and emerging trends that can contribute to your multiple income streams. Explore the impact of technology, the gig economy, and the sharing economy on creating innovative income-generating channels. Embrace a mindset of continuous learning and adaptability to identify and capitalize on emerging opportunities in the ever-evolving marketplace.

Conclusion:

As we conclude this chapter, you have gained a deeper understanding of the importance of multiple streams of income in your financial journey. By diversifying your income sources through active, passive, and portfolio income streams, you create a solid foundation for building wealth and financial independence. In the chapters ahead, we will further explore practical strategies and insights that will empower you to explore and create diverse income streams aligned with your skills, passions, and market demands. Get ready to embrace the concept of multiple income streams and unlock the wealth-building potential it holds for your financial future.

Chapter 6: Smart Money Management: Budgeting, Saving, and Debt Reduction

Introduction:

In this chapter, we dive into the realm of smart money management—a crucial aspect of achieving financial greatness. We explore the foundational pillars of budgeting, saving, and debt reduction, providing you with practical strategies to take control of your finances, build wealth, and create a solid financial future.

6.1 The Importance of Budgeting:

Understand the significance of budgeting as a tool for managing your finances effectively. Learn how to create a comprehensive budget that reflects your income, expenses, and financial goals. Explore budgeting methods such as the 50/30/20 rule, zero-based budgeting, and envelope system. Discover techniques for tracking and analyzing your expenses, identifying areas for potential savings, and aligning your spending with your financial priorities.

6.2 Saving Strategies and Emergency Funds:

Explore various saving strategies that enable you to accumulate wealth and create financial stability. Learn the art of setting saving goals, automating savings, and leveraging compound interest to accelerate your savings growth. Understand the importance of building an emergency fund to protect yourself from unexpected financial challenges. Discover practical tips for saving consistently and managing your savings effectively.

6.3 Debt Reduction and Management:

Develop strategies for reducing and managing debt to regain financial freedom. Understand the different types of debt and their impact on your financial well-being. Explore techniques for prioritizing and paying off debts, including the debt snowball and debt avalanche methods. Learn strategies for negotiating lower interest rates, consolidating debts, and managing credit wisely. Gain insights into long-term debt management and creating a plan to stay debt-free.

6.4 Investing for Long-Term Wealth:

Delve into the world of investing and discover how it can contribute to your long-term wealth-building goals. Learn about different investment vehicles, including stocks, bonds, mutual funds, and real estate. Understand the principles of diversification, risk tolerance, and long-term investing strategies. Explore techniques for evaluating investment opportunities, building a balanced investment portfolio, and leveraging the power of compounding to accelerate your wealth growth.

6.5 Financial Protection and Insurance:

Explore the importance of financial protection through insurance. Learn about different types of insurance, including health insurance, life insurance, and property insurance. Understand how insurance can safeguard your financial well-being and protect you from unforeseen circumstances. Discover techniques for evaluating insurance needs, choosing the right policies, and maximizing your coverage while managing costs.

6.6 Navigating Financial Challenges:

Develop resilience and adaptability in navigating financial challenges. Learn how to cope with unexpected expenses, income fluctuations, and economic downturns. Explore strategies for adjusting your budget, finding alternative income sources, and seeking professional guidance when needed. Develop a mindset that embraces financial challenges as opportunities for growth and learning.

Conclusion:

As we conclude this chapter, you have gained valuable insights into smart money management, including budgeting, saving, and debt reduction. By implementing these strategies, you are taking control of your financial destiny, building a solid foundation for wealth creation, and protecting yourself from financial uncertainties. In the chapters ahead, we will continue exploring practical strategies and insights that will empower you to optimize your money management practices and achieve financial greatness. Get ready to master the art of smart money management and pave the way for a prosperous and secure financial future.

Chapter 7: The Art of Investing: Building and Diversifying Your Portfolio

Introduction:

In Chapter 7, we delve into the art of investing—an essential pillar of wealth creation. We explore the strategies and principles that will help you build and diversify your investment portfolio, allowing you to capitalize on opportunities, mitigate risks, and achieve long-term financial growth.

7.1 Understanding Investment Basics:

We begin by laying a strong foundation in investment basics. Explore key concepts such as risk and return, asset classes, and investment vehicles. Understand the importance of setting clear investment goals and aligning your investment strategy with your financial objectives. Gain insights into different investment approaches, such as value investing, growth investing, and income investing, and how they can shape your investment decisions.

7.2 Building Your Investment Portfolio:

Learn how to build a well-balanced and diversified investment portfolio. Explore strategies for asset allocation, considering factors such as your risk tolerance, investment horizon, and financial goals. Understand the role of different asset classes, including stocks, bonds, real estate, and alternative investments, in creating a diversified portfolio. Gain insights into the advantages of diversification and its ability to mitigate risks while maximizing potential returns.

7.3 Investing in Stocks:

Delve into the world of stock market investing. Learn how to evaluate individual stocks, analyze financial statements, and assess company fundamentals. Understand different investment strategies, such as value investing, growth investing, and dividend investing, and how to apply them to your stock selection process. Explore techniques for portfolio diversification within the stock market and the importance of monitoring and managing your stock holdings.

7.4 Bond Investments and Fixed-Income Securities:

Explore the world of fixed-income investments and bonds. Understand the different types of bonds, including government bonds, corporate bonds, and municipal bonds, and their risk and return profiles. Learn how to evaluate bond investments, assess credit ratings, and analyze interest rate trends. Explore strategies for incorporating bonds into your investment portfolio, balancing risk and income generation.

7.5 Real Estate Investments:

Dive into the realm of real estate investments as a valuable addition to your portfolio. Learn about different real estate investment options, such as rental properties, real estate investment trusts (REITs), and crowdfunding platforms. Explore techniques for evaluating real estate opportunities, assessing property values, and understanding market dynamics. Gain insights into the advantages of real estate investments, including potential cash flow, appreciation, and portfolio diversification.

7.6 Alternative Investments and Portfolio Expansion:

Expand your investment horizons by exploring alternative investment opportunities. Learn about alternative assets, such as commodities, precious metals, cryptocurrencies, and private equity. Understand the unique characteristics and risks associated with these investments. Explore techniques for incorporating alternative investments into your portfolio to enhance diversification and potential returns.

Conclusion:

As we conclude this chapter, you have gained a deeper understanding of the art of investing and the importance of building and diversifying your investment portfolio. By aligning your investment strategy with your financial goals, diversifying across asset classes, and understanding the nuances of different investment options, you can navigate the complex world of investing with confidence. In the chapters ahead, we will continue to explore advanced investment strategies and insights that will empower you to optimize your investment portfolio and accelerate your journey towards financial greatness. Get ready to unleash the power of investing and unlock the potential for long-term wealth creation and financial independence.

Chapter 8: Entrepreneurship and Wealth Creation: From Ideas to Profitable Ventures

Introduction:

In Chapter 8, we embark on a journey into the world of entrepreneurship—a powerful pathway to wealth creation and financial freedom. We explore the mindset, skills, and strategies necessary to transform your ideas into profitable ventures. Whether you aspire to start your own business or innovate within existing organizations, this chapter will equip you with the tools to unleash your entrepreneurial potential.

8.1 The Entrepreneurial Mindset:

Develop an entrepreneurial mindset that fuels innovation, resilience, and a relentless pursuit of success. Explore the characteristics of successful entrepreneurs, such as risk-taking, perseverance, creativity, and adaptability. Gain insights into the importance of embracing failure as a learning opportunity and maintaining a growth mindset. Cultivate the passion and determination required to navigate the challenges and uncertainties of the entrepreneurial journey.

8.2 Ideation and Opportunity Recognition:

Discover techniques for generating and evaluating business ideas. Learn how to identify opportunities in the marketplace by observing trends, understanding customer needs, and analyzing industry gaps. Explore methodologies like brainstorming, problem-solving frameworks, and market research to refine your ideas and assess their viability. Understand the importance of market fit and differentiation in shaping your entrepreneurial ventures.

8.3 Business Planning and Execution:

Master the art of business planning and execution. Learn how to develop a comprehensive business plan that outlines your vision, mission, target market, competitive advantage, and financial projections. Explore strategies for resource allocation, team building, and operational excellence. Understand the significance of adaptability and continuous refinement in executing your business plans and staying ahead of market dynamics.

8.4 Financial Management for Entrepreneurs:

Gain a solid understanding of financial management principles for entrepreneurs. Explore concepts such as cash flow management, budgeting, financial forecasting, and raising capital. Learn techniques for pricing your products or services, managing expenses, and maximizing profitability. Understand the importance of financial literacy and leveraging financial tools and technologies to support your entrepreneurial endeavors.

8.5 Marketing and Branding Strategies:

Develop effective marketing and branding strategies to create awareness, attract customers, and build a strong brand presence. Explore techniques for market segmentation, targeting, and positioning. Learn how to craft compelling marketing messages, leverage digital marketing channels, and engage with your target audience. Understand the significance of customer relationship management and building long-term customer loyalty.

8.6 Scaling and Growth Strategies:

Unlock strategies for scaling and growing your entrepreneurial ventures. Explore techniques for expanding your customer base, entering new markets, and diversifying your product or service offerings. Learn about strategic partnerships, mergers and acquisitions, and franchising as avenues for growth. Understand the challenges and opportunities associated with scaling your business and develop a roadmap for sustainable expansion.

Conclusion:

As we conclude this chapter, you have gained valuable insights into entrepreneurship and its potential for wealth creation. By embracing the entrepreneurial mindset, recognizing opportunities, and executing sound business strategies, you can transform your ideas into profitable ventures. In the chapters ahead, we will continue to explore advanced entrepreneurial concepts, innovation frameworks, and success stories that will inspire and empower you on your entrepreneurial journey. Get ready to unleash your entrepreneurial spirit, seize opportunities, and create lasting wealth through the power of entrepreneurship.

Part III: Navigating Challenges and Adversity

Chapter 9: Resilience and Persistence: Overcoming Obstacles on Your Path to Wealth

Introduction:

In Chapter 9, we delve into the critical traits of resilience and persistence—essential qualities that enable individuals to overcome obstacles and achieve long-term success on their path to wealth. We explore strategies and mindset shifts that will empower you to navigate challenges, bounce back from setbacks, and stay focused on your financial goals.

9.1 Understanding Resilience:

Develop a deep understanding of resilience and its role in achieving wealth. Explore the characteristics of resilient individuals, such as adaptability, optimism, and emotional intelligence. Learn how to cultivate resilience by building a strong support network, practicing self-care, and embracing a growth mindset. Understand the importance of reframing challenges as opportunities for growth and developing coping mechanisms to thrive in the face of adversity.

9.2 Navigating Financial Setbacks:

Explore techniques for navigating financial setbacks and setbacks along your wealth-building journey. Learn how to effectively manage financial crises, such as job loss, economic downturns, or unexpected expenses. Discover strategies for creating emergency funds, managing debt, and adapting your financial plans in response to changing circumstances. Develop the ability to bounce back from setbacks and use them as stepping stones toward future success.

9.3 Overcoming Mental and Emotional Barriers:

Address mental and emotional barriers that can hinder your progress on the path to wealth. Learn techniques for managing fear, self-doubt, and limiting beliefs around money. Explore methods for building self-confidence and cultivating a positive mindset. Discover strategies for reframing failure, embracing feedback, and maintaining motivation during challenging times. Develop resilience in the face of criticism and learn to use it as fuel for personal growth.

9.4 Building a Supportive Network:

Recognize the power of a supportive network in overcoming obstacles and achieving financial greatness. Learn how to surround yourself with individuals who share your aspirations and values. Discover the importance of mentors, accountability partners, and like-minded communities. Explore strategies for building and nurturing relationships that foster collaboration, learning, and resilience.

9.5 Continuous Learning and Adaptability:

Embrace continuous learning and adaptability as key factors in overcoming obstacles on your wealth-building journey. Explore the importance of staying informed about market trends, industry shifts, and emerging opportunities. Develop a growth mindset that thrives on curiosity and seeks out new knowledge. Learn to adapt your strategies and approaches based on feedback, data, and changing circumstances. Embrace lifelong learning as a means to evolve and stay ahead in an ever-changing world.

9.6 Staying Focused on Your Financial Goals:

Develop strategies for staying focused on your financial goals despite distractions and setbacks. Learn techniques for setting clear goals, breaking them down into actionable steps, and tracking your progress. Explore ways to stay motivated and disciplined in your wealth-building efforts. Discover the power of visualization, affirmations, and accountability systems in maintaining focus and persistence. Develop a resilient mindset that keeps you aligned with your long-term financial vision.

Conclusion:

As we conclude this chapter, you have gained valuable insights into the importance of resilience and persistence in overcoming obstacles on your path to wealth. By embracing resilience, navigating setbacks, and staying focused on your financial goals, you have the power to overcome challenges and achieve long-term success. In the chapters ahead, we will continue to explore advanced strategies, success stories, and mindset shifts that will empower you to build unshakable resilience and persistence on your wealth-building journey. Get ready to embrace the power within you and forge ahead with determination and unwavering persistence toward your financial greatness.

Chapter 10: Embracing Risk: Calculated Moves for Financial Growth

Introduction:

In Chapter 10, we delve into the realm of risk and its role in achieving financial growth. We explore the concept of calculated risk-taking and how it can propel you towards greater wealth. By understanding and effectively managing risks, you can seize opportunities, diversify your portfolio, and unlock new avenues for financial success.

10.1 The Nature of Risk:

Gain a comprehensive understanding of risk and its relationship with financial growth. Explore different types of risks, including market risk, business risk, and personal risk. Understand the impact of risk on investment decisions, entrepreneurship, and wealth-building strategies. Learn to differentiate between calculated risks and reckless behavior, developing a discerning mindset that evaluates risk-reward trade-offs.

10.2 Risk Assessment and Analysis:

Develop techniques for assessing and analyzing risks in various contexts. Learn to identify potential risks and their potential impact on your financial goals. Explore risk assessment frameworks, such as SWOT analysis (Strengths, Weaknesses, Opportunities, and Threats) and scenario planning, to evaluate and mitigate risks. Understand the importance of conducting thorough research, seeking expert advice, and leveraging data to inform your risk management decisions.

10.3 Building a Risk-Tolerant Mindset:

Cultivate a risk-tolerant mindset that embraces uncertainty and seeks opportunities for growth. Understand the psychological factors that influence risk tolerance, such as fear, loss aversion, and cognitive biases. Learn strategies to manage emotional responses to risk, including reframing, rational decision-making, and building resilience. Develop the ability to assess and manage risk within your comfort level while pushing the boundaries of your risk tolerance.

10.4 Diversification and Risk Management:

Explore the power of diversification as a risk management strategy. Learn how to diversify your investment portfolio across different asset classes, industries, and geographic regions. Understand the principles of correlation, asset allocation, and risk-adjusted returns in building a diversified portfolio. Explore techniques for managing risks within specific investments, such as hedging strategies and portfolio rebalancing. Gain insights into risk management tools, such as stop-loss orders and insurance products.

10.5 Evaluating High-Reward Opportunities:

Navigate the landscape of high-reward opportunities while effectively managing associated risks. Learn to identify potential high-reward investments, business ventures, or career opportunities. Explore due diligence processes, financial analysis, and market research techniques to assess the feasibility and potential returns of these opportunities. Understand the importance of understanding and managing downside risks while maximizing upside potential.

10.6 Risk Mitigation Strategies:

Develop risk mitigation strategies to protect your financial interests and minimize potential losses. Explore techniques such as setting up emergency funds, insurance coverage, and legal protections. Learn about contingency planning, risk transfer mechanisms, and negotiation strategies. Develop resilience and adaptability to respond to unforeseen risks and recover from potential setbacks.

Conclusion:

As we conclude this chapter, you have gained a deeper understanding of embracing risk and its role in financial growth. By developing a calculated approach to risk-taking, conducting thorough risk assessments, and implementing risk mitigation strategies, you can navigate the complex landscape of risk while unlocking opportunities for financial success. In the chapters ahead, we will continue to explore advanced risk management techniques, case studies, and success stories that will empower you to make informed decisions and embrace risk strategically on your journey to financial greatness. Get ready to step outside your comfort zone, embrace calculated risks, and propel yourself towards greater financial growth and abundance.

Chapter 11: Learning from Failure: Transforming Setbacks into Opportunities

Introduction:

In Chapter 11, we delve into the invaluable lessons that can be learned from failure and setbacks on the path to financial success. We explore the mindset, strategies, and resilience required to transform setbacks into opportunities for growth and advancement. By embracing failure as a catalyst for learning and personal development, you can navigate challenges with resilience, adaptability, and unwavering determination.

11.1 Embracing a Growth Mindset:

Understand the power of a growth mindset in the face of failure. Explore the concept of fixed mindset versus growth mindset and learn to cultivate a belief in the ability to learn, adapt, and improve. Discover the mindset shifts necessary to view failures as stepping stones to success, rather than indicators of personal shortcomings. Develop resilience, optimism, and a willingness to take calculated risks as you embark on your journey of turning setbacks into opportunities.

11.2 Analyzing Failure and Extracting Lessons:

Learn how to effectively analyze failure and extract valuable lessons from it. Explore techniques for conducting post-mortem evaluations, identifying root causes, and understanding the factors that contributed to the setback. Gain insights into the importance of honest self-reflection, seeking feedback, and learning from mistakes. Develop a systematic approach to evaluating failures and extracting actionable insights that will guide your future decisions and actions.

11.3 Building Resilience and Bouncing Back:

Develop strategies for building resilience and bouncing back from failure. Discover techniques for managing emotions, processing setbacks, and maintaining mental and emotional well-being during challenging times. Explore the power of self-care, support systems, and positive affirmations in cultivating resilience. Learn to reframe failures as learning opportunities, allowing them to fuel your determination and drive to achieve financial success.

11.4 Iterative Approach and Continuous Improvement:

Embrace the iterative approach and continuous improvement mindset as you learn from failure. Explore the concept of rapid experimentation, incremental progress, and course correction. Understand the value of agility, adaptability, and flexibility in responding to setbacks and adjusting your strategies. Discover techniques for setting achievable goals, monitoring progress, and making data-informed decisions to continuously refine and improve your financial journey.

11.5 Innovation and Creativity as a Response to Failure:

Harness the power of innovation and creativity as a response to failure. Explore how setbacks can spur innovative thinking, new ideas, and unconventional approaches. Learn techniques for fostering a culture of creativity, embracing curiosity, and challenging the status quo. Discover how innovation can lead to breakthroughs, differentiation, and competitive advantage in your wealth-building pursuits.

11.6 Turning Setbacks into Opportunities:

Master the art of turning setbacks into opportunities for growth and advancement. Explore examples of individuals who have transformed failure into success, leveraging their experiences to propel themselves forward. Learn strategies for reframing setbacks, adapting your approach, and seizing new opportunities that arise from failure. Develop the resilience and mindset necessary to bounce back stronger and more determined to achieve your financial goals.

Conclusion:

As we conclude this chapter, you have gained valuable insights into the transformative power of learning from failure and setbacks on your path to financial success. By embracing a growth mindset, analyzing failures, building resilience, and fostering innovation, you have the ability to transform setbacks into stepping stones towards greater opportunities. In the chapters ahead, we will continue to explore advanced strategies, success stories, and resilience-building techniques that will empower you to thrive in the face of adversity and unlock your full potential. Get ready to embrace failures as valuable teachers, learn from them, and emerge stronger, wiser, and more determined to achieve financial greatness.

Chapter 12: Building a Support Network: Surrounding Yourself with Like-Minded Individuals

Introduction:

In Chapter 12, we explore the importance of building a supportive network on your journey to financial success. Surrounding yourself with like-minded individuals who share your aspirations, values, and drive can significantly impact your mindset, motivation, and opportunities. We delve into strategies for cultivating meaningful relationships, seeking mentorship, and tapping into the power of collaboration and community.

12.1 Recognizing the Power of a Supportive Network:

Understand the transformative power of a supportive network in your pursuit of financial success. Explore how being surrounded by like-minded individuals can boost motivation, provide encouragement, and foster a sense of accountability. Learn the advantages of networking, collaborating, and sharing experiences with others who are on a similar path. Recognize that success is not a solitary journey but one that is enhanced through meaningful connections.

12.2 Identifying Your Support Network:

Assess your existing network and identify gaps that need to be filled. Explore techniques for finding and connecting with like-minded individuals who align with your financial goals and values. Discover different avenues for expanding your network, such as professional associations, industry events, online communities, and mentorship programs. Understand the importance of diversity within your network to gain diverse perspectives, knowledge, and opportunities.

12.3 Cultivating Meaningful Relationships:

Learn strategies for cultivating meaningful relationships within your support network. Develop effective communication skills, active listening, and empathy. Explore techniques for building rapport, trust, and mutual respect with individuals who can support and inspire you. Discover the art of giving and receiving support, advice, and constructive feedback within your network. Foster a culture of collaboration, reciprocity, and shared learning.

12.4 Seeking Mentorship and Role Models:

Recognize the value of mentorship and the guidance of role models in your financial journey. Explore ways to identify potential mentors and role models who have achieved success in areas you aspire to. Learn how to approach and engage mentors, seeking their advice, insights, and wisdom. Understand the importance of mentorship in gaining perspective, learning from others' experiences, and avoiding common pitfalls.

12.5 Collaborating for Success:

Harness the power of collaboration within your support network. Explore opportunities for joint ventures, partnerships, and shared projects that can accelerate your progress. Understand the benefits of pooling resources, expertise, and networks to achieve shared goals. Discover how collaborative efforts can lead to innovation, growth, and expanded opportunities for financial success. Cultivate a mindset of abundance and collaboration within your network.

12.6 Nurturing and Sustaining Your Network:

Learn techniques for nurturing and sustaining your support

network over the long term. Understand the importance of regular communication, maintaining connections, and expressing gratitude. Explore strategies for providing value and support to others in your network. Embrace the concept of paying it forward, recognizing that the success of your network is intertwined with your own success. Cultivate a culture of reciprocity, encouragement, and collective growth.

Conclusion:

As we conclude this chapter, you have gained a deeper understanding of the significance of building a supportive network on your journey to financial success. By surrounding yourself with like-minded individuals, seeking mentorship, and embracing collaboration, you can leverage the collective wisdom, support, and opportunities within your network. In the chapters ahead, we will continue to explore advanced networking strategies, success stories, and techniques for fostering meaningful connections. Get ready to expand your network, tap into the power of collective intelligence, and accelerate your progress on the path to financial greatness.

Part IV: Maximizing Opportunities

Chapter 13: Identifying Lucrative Trends and Markets: The Power of Research and Analysis

Introduction:

In Chapter 13, we delve into the critical skill of identifying lucrative trends and markets in your pursuit of financial success. Understanding how to conduct thorough research and analysis allows you to uncover emerging opportunities, capitalize on market shifts, and stay ahead of the curve. We explore effective strategies, tools, and techniques for conducting market research, trend analysis, and evaluating the potential profitability of various industries.

13.1 The Importance of Market Research:

Understand the significance of market research in identifying lucrative trends and markets. Learn the fundamentals of market research, including primary and secondary research methods, data collection techniques, and analysis. Explore the role of market research in identifying customer needs, understanding competitive landscapes, and making informed business decisions. Gain insights into the power of market research in reducing risks and maximizing the potential for financial success.

13.2 Conducting Industry Analysis:

Develop the skills to conduct comprehensive industry analysis. Learn techniques for evaluating industry trends, competitive dynamics, and growth potential. Explore tools such as Porter's Five Forces analysis, SWOT analysis (Strengths, Weaknesses, Opportunities, and Threats), and market sizing. Understand the importance of studying industry trends, technological advancements, regulatory landscapes, and consumer behavior to identify lucrative markets.

13.3 Identifying Emerging Trends:

Discover strategies for identifying emerging trends that can lead to financial opportunities. Learn to monitor social, economic, technological, and cultural changes that shape consumer demands and market dynamics. Explore techniques for trend spotting, including trend analysis, observing consumer behavior, and staying up-to-date with industry publications and thought leaders. Develop the ability to identify early signals of emerging trends and position yourself to capitalize on them.

13.4 Evaluating Market Potential:

Gain insights into evaluating the potential profitability of different markets. Understand key metrics, such as market size, growth rate, and target market demographics. Explore techniques for analyzing market demand, competition, and barriers to entry. Learn to assess market saturation, market dynamics, and customer segments to identify untapped opportunities. Develop a systematic approach for evaluating market potential and selecting the most promising avenues for financial success.

13.5 Leveraging Technology and Data:

Harness the power of technology and data in identifying lucrative trends and markets. Explore the role of artificial intelligence, big data analytics, and predictive modeling in market research and trend analysis. Discover tools and platforms that provide valuable insights and automate data collection and analysis processes. Understand the importance of data-driven decision-making and leveraging technology to gain a competitive edge in identifying and capitalizing on lucrative opportunities.

13.6 Adapting to Changing Market Landscapes:

Develop the agility and adaptability to navigate changing market landscapes. Understand that trends and markets evolve over time, and staying ahead requires continuous monitoring, learning, and adaptation. Learn techniques for staying attuned to market shifts, adapting your strategies, and embracing innovation. Cultivate a mindset that embraces change and sees it as an opportunity rather than a threat.

Conclusion:

As we conclude this chapter, you have gained valuable knowledge and skills in identifying lucrative trends and markets through research and analysis. By mastering the art of market research, conducting industry analysis, and staying attuned to emerging trends, you can position yourself for financial success. In the chapters ahead, we will continue to explore advanced strategies, case studies, and real-world examples that will sharpen your ability to identify and capitalize on lucrative opportunities. Get ready to dive deeper into the world of trends and markets, equip yourself with the necessary research and analytical skills, and seize the potential for financial greatness.

Chapter 14: Seizing Opportunities: Timing, Preparation, and Action

Introduction:

In Chapter 14, we explore the art of seizing opportunities on your path to financial success. Recognizing and capitalizing on opportunities requires a combination of timing, preparation, and decisive action. We delve into the mindset, strategies, and techniques necessary to identify and seize opportunities when they arise, allowing you to propel your wealth-building journey forward.

14.1 The Power of Timing:

Understand the significance of timing in seizing opportunities. Explore the concept of being in the right place at the right time and how it can lead to extraordinary financial gains. Learn techniques for developing a keen sense of timing, including market research, trend analysis, and staying attuned to industry dynamics. Discover the art of anticipating future opportunities and positioning yourself to take advantage of them when the timing is optimal.

14.2 Preparation: Building a Strong Foundation:

Develop the necessary preparation to seize opportunities when they present themselves. Explore the importance of continuous learning, skill development, and expanding your knowledge base. Learn techniques for building a strong foundation in areas relevant to your financial goals. Understand the value of cultivating a diverse skill set, developing expertise, and staying informed about emerging trends. Prepare yourself mentally, emotionally, and intellectually to be ready for the opportunities that come your way.

14.3 Recognizing Opportunities:

Sharpen your ability to recognize opportunities amidst the noise and complexity of the financial landscape. Learn techniques for identifying signals, patterns, and shifts that indicate potential opportunities. Explore the power of observation, intuition, and research in uncovering hidden gems. Develop the ability to think critically, question assumptions, and challenge conventional wisdom to identify overlooked opportunities. Cultivate a mindset that is open to new possibilities and receptive to unconventional ideas.

14.4 Taking Decisive Action:

Learn to take decisive action when opportunities arise. Understand the importance of overcoming fear, doubt, and analysis paralysis. Explore techniques for evaluating risks, making calculated decisions, and seizing opportunities with confidence. Develop strategies for effective decision-making, setting clear goals, and executing plans of action. Embrace a mindset of action and resourcefulness, understanding that opportunities are not passive occurrences but outcomes of proactive effort.

14.5 Mitigating Risks and Managing Uncertainty:

Understand the risks associated with seizing opportunities and develop strategies for mitigating them. Learn techniques for conducting risk assessments, contingency planning, and managing uncertainty. Explore the concept of calculated risk-taking and developing risk mitigation strategies. Understand the importance of diversification, maintaining a financial safety net, and seeking expert advice when necessary. Cultivate the ability to navigate uncertainties and make informed decisions that balance potential rewards with manageable risks.

14.6 Learning from Missed Opportunities:

Embrace the lessons that missed opportunities can teach you. Understand that setbacks and missed chances are part of the journey to financial success. Learn techniques for reflecting on missed opportunities, extracting valuable insights, and applying them to future endeavors. Develop resilience, adaptability, and a growth mindset that allows you to learn from setbacks and course-correct your path. Cultivate the ability to bounce back stronger and more determined to seize the next opportunity that comes your way.

Conclusion:

As we conclude this chapter, you have gained valuable insights into seizing opportunities on your path to financial success. By mastering the art of timing, preparation, and decisive action, you can position yourself to capitalize on the opportunities that arise. In the chapters ahead, we will continue to explore advanced strategies, success stories, and techniques for seizing opportunities in diverse contexts. Get ready to sharpen your ability to recognize, evaluate, and act upon opportunities, propelling yourself forward on the journey to financial greatness.

Chapter 15: Networking and Strategic Relationships: Opening Doors to Success

Introduction:

In Chapter 15, we delve into the power of networking and strategic relationships on your path to financial success. Building a strong network and cultivating strategic relationships can open doors to new opportunities, collaborations, and valuable resources. We explore the art of effective networking, relationship building, and leveraging connections to propel your journey towards wealth and achievement.

15.1 The Power of Networking:

Understand the transformative power of networking in your pursuit of financial success. Learn the fundamentals of effective networking, including building genuine connections, nurturing relationships, and creating mutually beneficial partnerships. Explore the various platforms and avenues for networking, both online and offline, and the opportunities they present. Discover the benefits of expanding your network, gaining access to valuable information, and tapping into a diverse pool of knowledge and resources.

15.2 Building Meaningful Connections:

Develop the skills to build meaningful connections that go beyond surface-level interactions. Understand the importance of authenticity, trust, and rapport in developing strong relationships. Learn techniques for effective communication, active listening, and fostering genuine connections with individuals in your network. Explore strategies for nurturing relationships over time, staying in touch, and providing value to others. Cultivate a mindset of generosity, collaboration, and mutual support within your network.

15.3 Strategic Relationship Building:

Recognize the power of strategic relationships in your journey to financial success. Explore the concept of identifying key stakeholders, influencers, and decision-makers in your industry or field. Learn techniques for approaching and developing relationships with strategic partners, mentors, and sponsors who can provide guidance, support, and opportunities. Understand the importance of aligning your goals, values, and aspirations with those of your strategic relationships for maximum impact.

15.4 Leveraging Your Network:

Discover strategies for leveraging your network to unlock new opportunities and accelerate your progress. Explore techniques for tapping into the collective knowledge, resources, and connections within your network. Learn how to seek advice, feedback, and guidance from trusted individuals in your network. Understand the power of referrals, endorsements, and collaborative ventures that can result from strong relationships. Develop the ability to leverage your network for introductions, partnerships, and access to new markets or opportunities.

15.5 Cultivating an Online Presence:

Understand the importance of cultivating an online presence in today's digital world. Explore the role of social media platforms, professional networking sites, and online communities in expanding your network and reaching a wider audience. Learn strategies for building a personal brand, sharing valuable content, and engaging with others in your industry or field. Discover the power of online networking events, webinars, and virtual conferences in expanding your network beyond geographical limitations.

15.6 Navigating Professional Associations and Industry Events:

Explore the opportunities presented by professional associations and industry events. Understand the importance of joining relevant associations and attending conferences, trade shows, and seminars. Learn techniques for making the most of these events, including effective networking, showcasing your expertise, and staying updated with industry trends. Discover the potential for collaboration, partnerships, and business opportunities that can arise from active participation in professional associations and industry events.

Conclusion:

As we conclude this chapter, you have gained a deeper understanding of the power of networking and strategic relationships on your journey to financial success. By building meaningful connections, cultivating strategic relationships, and leveraging your network, you can open doors to new opportunities, collaborations, and valuable resources. In the chapters ahead, we will continue to explore advanced networking strategies, success stories, and techniques for navigating the complex world of professional relationships. Get ready to expand your network, forge meaningful connections, and unlock the potential for financial greatness through strategic relationships.

Chapter 16: Innovation and Adaptability: Thriving in a Dynamic Financial Landscape

Introduction:

In Chapter 16, we explore the critical skills of innovation and adaptability in navigating the ever-changing financial landscape. In a world of rapid technological advancements, shifting consumer demands, and disruptive market forces, the ability to innovate and adapt is paramount for sustained financial success. We delve into strategies, mindsets, and practices that empower you to embrace change, foster innovation, and thrive amidst uncertainty.

16.1 Embracing a Culture of Innovation:

Understand the importance of fostering a culture of innovation in your financial pursuits. Explore the mindset and attitudes necessary to embrace innovation and think creatively. Learn techniques for cultivating an environment that encourages experimentation, risk-taking, and learning from failures. Discover the power of fostering a diverse and inclusive workforce, promoting collaboration, and embracing new ideas. Cultivate the ability to challenge the status quo and seek innovative solutions to financial challenges.

16.2 The Power of Disruption:

Recognize the opportunities that come with disruptive forces in the financial landscape. Understand that disruptions can create new markets, reshape industries, and present avenues for growth. Learn techniques for identifying disruptive trends and technologies that have the potential to revolutionize the way we do business. Explore case studies of successful disruptors and understand the principles behind their innovative approaches. Develop the ability to leverage disruptions to your advantage and proactively seek opportunities for innovation.

16.3 Nurturing a Growth Mindset:

Develop a growth mindset that fuels innovation and adaptation. Understand the importance of embracing continuous learning, seeking feedback, and embracing challenges. Learn techniques for overcoming fear of failure, reframing setbacks as learning opportunities, and developing resilience. Cultivate a mindset that sees obstacles as stepping stones to success and views change as an opportunity for growth. Foster an attitude of curiosity, experimentation, and continuous improvement in your financial endeavors.

16.4 Agile Strategies and Lean Thinking:

Explore agile strategies and lean thinking as tools for innovation and adaptation. Understand the principles of agile methodologies and how they can be applied to financial decision-making, project management, and problem-solving. Learn techniques for rapid experimentation, iterative development, and customer feedback loops. Discover the power of lean thinking in eliminating waste, optimizing processes, and creating value for customers. Develop the ability to embrace agility and lean practices to respond effectively to changing market dynamics.

16.5 Collaboration and Partnerships:

Recognize the value of collaboration and partnerships in fostering innovation and adaptation. Understand the power of diverse perspectives, collective intelligence, and collaborative problem-solving. Learn techniques for forging strategic alliances, joint ventures, and partnerships that amplify your innovative capabilities. Explore the benefits of cross-industry collaboration, open innovation, and ecosystem thinking. Develop the ability to build collaborative networks, leverage external expertise, and co-create innovative solutions.

16.6 Anticipating and Leading Change:

Develop the foresight and leadership skills necessary to anticipate and lead change in the financial landscape. Understand the importance of scanning the external environment, monitoring trends, and anticipating future shifts. Learn techniques for scenario planning, trend analysis, and strategic foresight. Explore the role of visionary leadership in guiding organizations through turbulent times. Cultivate the ability to navigate uncertainty, inspire others, and lead with agility and resilience in the face of change.

Conclusion:

As we conclude this chapter, you have gained valuable insights into the skills of innovation and adaptability in the dynamic financial landscape. By fostering a culture of innovation, embracing disruption, nurturing a growth mindset, and leveraging agile strategies, you can thrive amidst uncertainty and drive financial success. In the chapters ahead, we will continue to explore advanced strategies, real-world examples, and case studies that exemplify the power of innovation and adaptability in the pursuit of financial greatness. Get ready to embrace change, foster innovation, and position yourself as a leader in the dynamic financial landscape.

Part V: Living a Life of Wealth and Purpose

Chapter 17: Financial Freedom and Lifestyle Design: Creating the Life You Desire

Introduction:

In Chapter 17, we delve into the concept of financial freedom and lifestyle design, where your financial resources are aligned with your personal values and aspirations. We explore strategies, mindsets, and practices that empower you to create a life of abundance, purpose, and fulfillment. By understanding the principles of financial freedom and intentionally designing your lifestyle, you can shape your financial journey to support the life you desire.

17.1 Defining Financial Freedom:

Explore the meaning of financial freedom and its significance in shaping your lifestyle. Understand that financial freedom extends beyond accumulating wealth and focuses on achieving a state of financial well-being and security. Learn techniques for defining what financial freedom means to you personally, taking into account your goals, values, and desired lifestyle. Discover the connection between financial freedom and overall life satisfaction.

17.2 Clarifying Your Life Vision:

Develop a clear vision for the life you desire. Understand the importance of aligning your financial goals with your broader life goals and aspirations. Learn techniques for clarifying your values, identifying your passions, and determining what truly matters to you. Explore strategies for creating a compelling vision that serves as a guiding compass for your financial decisions.

Develop the ability to articulate your life vision with clarity and conviction.

17.3 Designing Your Lifestyle:

Take an intentional approach to designing your lifestyle based on your financial resources and personal preferences. Explore techniques for assessing your current lifestyle and identifying areas for improvement or alignment. Learn strategies for prioritizing your spending, distinguishing between needs and wants, and aligning your financial choices with your values and goals. Discover the power of minimalism, conscious consumption, and mindful spending in designing a lifestyle that brings you joy and fulfillment.

17.4 Creating Multiple Income Streams:

Diversify your income streams to support your desired lifestyle and financial freedom. Explore techniques for identifying opportunities for additional income, such as side hustles, freelance work, or investment ventures. Learn strategies for leveraging your skills, passions, and assets to generate multiple streams of income. Understand the benefits of creating passive income streams and developing assets that can generate ongoing revenue. Develop the mindset of an entrepreneur, embracing the possibilities of financial abundance through multiple income streams.

17.5 Financial Planning for Your Desired Lifestyle:

Develop a comprehensive financial plan that aligns with your desired lifestyle. Learn techniques for budgeting, saving, and investing in a way that supports your life vision. Explore strategies for managing debt, optimizing your cash flow, and building a solid financial foundation. Understand the importance of setting clear financial goals, tracking your progress, and making adjustments along the way. Develop the ability to make informed financial decisions that are in alignment with your desired lifestyle.

17.6 Balancing Work and Life:

Achieving financial freedom is not just about accumulating wealth but also about creating a balance between work and life. Explore techniques for time management, prioritization, and boundary setting to ensure that your lifestyle is not solely focused on financial pursuits. Learn strategies for cultivating meaningful relationships, pursuing hobbies and interests, and maintaining overall well-being. Discover the power of self-care, rest, and rejuvenation in sustaining a fulfilling and balanced lifestyle.

Conclusion:

As we conclude this chapter, you have gained insights into the concept of financial freedom and lifestyle design. By defining financial freedom on your terms, clarifying your life vision, designing your lifestyle, and creating multiple income streams, you can create the life you desire. In the chapters ahead, we will continue to explore advanced strategies, success stories, and techniques for achieving financial freedom and designing a life of abundance and purpose. Get ready to align your financial resources with your aspirations and create a life that brings you joy, fulfillment, and freedom.

Chapter 18: Giving Back and Impact: Using Wealth to Make a Difference

Introduction:

In Chapter 18, we explore the power of giving back and making a positive impact with your wealth. As you strive for financial success, it is essential to consider how you can use your resources to create meaningful change in the world. We delve into the principles of philanthropy, social responsibility, and conscious giving. By understanding the importance of giving back and leveraging your wealth for the greater good, you can leave a lasting legacy and make a difference in the lives of others.

18.1 The Meaning and Benefits of Giving:

Understand the meaning of giving back and its impact on your personal well-being and fulfillment. Explore the benefits of philanthropy, including increased happiness, a sense of purpose, and strengthened connections with others. Learn about the different ways you can give, whether through financial contributions, volunteering, or sharing your expertise. Discover the transformative power of giving and the positive ripple effects it can create in communities and society as a whole.

18.2 Finding Your Philanthropic Passion:

Identify your philanthropic passion and the causes that resonate with you. Explore techniques for discovering your values, interests, and areas of impact. Learn how to align your philanthropic efforts with your personal mission and values. Understand the importance of focusing your giving on areas where you can make a meaningful difference. Discover the joy and fulfillment that comes from supporting causes that are close to your heart.

18.3 Strategic Giving and Impact Investing:

Develop a strategic approach to your giving by considering the impact and effectiveness of your contributions. Learn about impact investing, a powerful tool that combines financial returns with positive social and environmental outcomes. Explore techniques for conducting due diligence on charitable organizations and social enterprises to ensure that your resources are used effectively. Discover the potential for creating sustainable change through strategic giving and impact investing.

18.4 Engaging in Corporate Social Responsibility:

If you are a business owner or leader, understand the importance of corporate social responsibility (CSR) and how it can contribute to your company's success and reputation. Learn about integrating social and environmental initiatives into your business practices. Explore strategies for aligning your company's values with its philanthropic efforts. Discover the potential for creating positive social impact through your business operations, supply chain practices, and employee engagement.

18.5 Building Collaborative Partnerships:

Recognize the power of collaborative partnerships in maximizing the impact of your philanthropic efforts. Learn about the benefits of collaborating with other individuals, organizations, and communities to address complex social challenges. Explore techniques for building effective partnerships, fostering trust, and leveraging collective resources. Discover the potential for collaborative initiatives that create systemic change and address root causes of social issues.

18.6 Leaving a Lasting Legacy:

Consider the legacy you want to leave through your philanthropic efforts. Explore techniques for creating a long-term impact by establishing foundations, endowments, or charitable trusts. Learn about estate planning and incorporating philanthropy into your financial legacy. Discover the joy and fulfillment that comes from knowing your wealth will continue to make a positive difference in the lives of others for generations to come.

Conclusion:

As we conclude this chapter, you have gained insights into the power of giving back and using your wealth to make a difference. By finding your philanthropic passion, engaging in strategic giving, embracing corporate social responsibility, building collaborative partnerships, and leaving a lasting legacy, you can create a positive impact in the world. In the final chapters ahead, we will explore advanced strategies, inspiring stories, and practical tools for maximizing your impact and creating a legacy of positive change. Get ready to make a difference and leave a lasting imprint on the world through your generous spirit and meaningful contributions.

Chapter 19: Legacy Building: Leaving a Lasting Financial and Emotional Heritage

Introduction:

In Chapter 19, we delve into the concept of legacy building and the importance of creating a lasting financial and emotional heritage. As you strive for financial greatness, it is crucial to consider the impact you will have beyond your own lifetime. We explore strategies, mindsets, and practices that empower you to shape your legacy, leaving a positive imprint on future generations. By intentionally building a legacy that encompasses both financial and emotional aspects, you can create a lasting impact that transcends mere wealth accumulation.

19.1 Defining Your Legacy:

Understand the meaning and significance of legacy and its impact on future generations. Reflect on what you want to be remembered for and the values you want to pass on. Learn techniques for clarifying your legacy vision, setting meaningful goals, and aligning your actions with your desired impact. Explore the power of storytelling and the role it plays in shaping your legacy narrative.

19.2 Financial Legacy Planning:

Develop a comprehensive financial legacy plan that aligns with your values and goals. Learn strategies for effective estate planning, including wills, trusts, and asset distribution. Understand the importance of tax planning and minimizing the financial burden on your beneficiaries. Explore techniques for passing on financial knowledge and wisdom to future generations, promoting responsible wealth management, and fostering a sense of stewardship.

19.3 Philanthropic Legacy:

Explore the role of philanthropy in shaping your legacy. Learn about charitable giving strategies, establishing foundations, and creating impact through donations. Understand the importance of involving your family in philanthropic endeavors and instilling a sense of social responsibility. Explore techniques for engaging your loved ones in philanthropic decision-making and fostering a culture of giving that extends beyond your lifetime.

19.4 Emotional Legacy:

Recognize the significance of your emotional legacy and the impact it has on your loved ones. Explore techniques for nurturing meaningful relationships, fostering open communication, and leaving a legacy of love, kindness, and respect. Learn strategies for passing on family values, traditions, and stories that connect generations. Understand the importance of documenting your personal history and preserving your family's legacy for future generations.

19.5 Mentorship and Succession Planning:

Develop a mentorship and succession plan to ensure the continuity of your legacy. Learn techniques for identifying and mentoring future leaders within your family or organization. Explore strategies for effective succession planning, including grooming successors, transferring knowledge and expertise, and ensuring a smooth transition. Understand the importance of empowering the next generation to carry forward your values and vision.

19.6 Living Your Legacy Today:

Recognize that your legacy is not something reserved for the future—it is something you can actively live and cultivate today. Explore techniques for aligning your actions and decisions with your legacy vision. Embrace the power of intentional living, mindfulness, and self-reflection in shaping your legacy. Discover the joy and fulfillment that comes from knowing you are making a positive impact and leaving a meaningful heritage.

Conclusion:

As we conclude this chapter, you have gained insights into the importance of legacy building and creating a lasting financial and emotional heritage. By defining your legacy, engaging in financial legacy planning, fostering a philanthropic legacy, nurturing an emotional legacy, embracing mentorship and succession planning, and living your legacy today, you can shape a legacy that transcends mere financial wealth. In the final chapter ahead, we will reflect on your journey towards financial greatness and provide key takeaways to guide you as you continue to build a legacy that will impact future generations. Get ready to leave a lasting imprint and make a difference that will be remembered for years to come.

Chapter 20: The Journey Continues: Sustaining Your Millionaire Mindset

Introduction:

In Chapter 20, we acknowledge that the path to financial greatness is not a destination but an ongoing journey. Sustaining your millionaire mindset is essential for long-term success and fulfillment. We explore strategies, habits, and practices that will help you stay motivated, resilient, and focused on your financial goals. By embracing continuous growth, adapting to change, and nurturing your mindset, you can ensure that your journey towards financial greatness is a lifelong pursuit.

20.1 Embracing Continuous Learning:

Understand the importance of lifelong learning in sustaining your millionaire mindset. Explore techniques for expanding your knowledge, acquiring new skills, and staying abreast of industry trends. Discover the power of reading books, attending seminars, engaging in online courses, and seeking mentorship as ways to enhance your expertise. Embrace curiosity and a growth mindset, always seeking opportunities for personal and professional development.

20.2 Staying Motivated and Goal-Oriented:

Maintain your motivation and focus on your financial goals throughout your journey. Learn techniques for setting clear and measurable goals that align with your vision. Explore strategies for breaking down your goals into actionable steps and creating a plan for their achievement. Discover the power of visualization, affirmations, and positive self-talk in maintaining a high level of motivation and commitment.

20.3 Navigating Challenges and Embracing Resilience:

Acknowledge that challenges and setbacks are a natural part of the journey. Learn techniques for building resilience, bouncing back from failure, and adapting to change. Explore strategies for reframing obstacles as opportunities for growth and learning. Discover the importance of maintaining a positive mindset, seeking support from mentors or a mastermind group, and persevering through difficult times.

20.4 Balancing Ambition and Well-Being:

Recognize the significance of maintaining a balance between your ambition for financial success and your overall well-being. Explore techniques for managing stress, practicing self-care, and nurturing your physical and mental health. Understand the importance of setting boundaries, prioritizing your time, and cultivating meaningful relationships. Discover the power of mindfulness, meditation, and gratitude in maintaining a sense of balance and fulfillment.

20.5 Giving Back and Paying It Forward:

Continue to embrace the spirit of giving back and making a positive impact as you sustain your millionaire mindset. Explore techniques for incorporating philanthropy and acts of kindness into your daily life. Discover the fulfillment that comes from sharing your knowledge, resources, and time with others. Understand the importance of using your success to uplift and inspire those around you.

20.6 Celebrating Milestones and Reflecting on Your Journey:

Take the time to celebrate your achievements and milestones along the way. Reflect on how far you have come and the lessons you have learned. Explore techniques for journaling, self-reflection, and gratitude practices that help you appreciate your progress. Embrace a mindset of abundance and celebrate not only your financial success but also the personal growth and positive impact you have made.

Conclusion:

As we conclude this chapter, we recognize that the journey towards financial greatness is a lifelong endeavor. By embracing continuous learning, staying motivated and goal-oriented, navigating challenges with resilience, balancing ambition and well-being, giving back and paying it forward, and celebrating milestones, you can sustain your millionaire mindset and continue to grow and thrive. Remember that the journey is not just about accumulating wealth, but also about personal growth, fulfillment, and making a positive impact on the world. May your journey continue to inspire and empower you as you create a life of abundance and significance.

Conclusion: Your Path to Financial Greatness

As we reach the conclusion of this book, it is important to reflect on the incredible journey you have embarked upon—the path to financial greatness. Throughout these pages, we have explored the mindset, strategies, and actions necessary to achieve extraordinary financial success. You have delved into the depths of your relationship with money, cultivated a wealth mindset, and rewired your subconscious for success. You have learned the power of goal setting, visualization, and manifesting your financial dreams.

We have explored the importance of multiple streams of income, smart money management, and building a diversified investment portfolio. You have gained insights into the world of entrepreneurship, risk-taking, and learning from failure. We have discussed the significance of building a strong support network, identifying lucrative trends, and seizing opportunities.

You have explored the principles of resilience, embracing risk, and the art of strategic relationships. We have discussed the value of innovation, adaptability, and designing a lifestyle that aligns with your financial aspirations. And, most importantly, we have delved into the power of giving back and using your wealth to make a difference.

Throughout this journey, you have acquired a wealth of knowledge, tools, and inspiration. You have cultivated a millionaire mindset and developed the skills necessary to navigate the ever-changing financial landscape. You are equipped with the strategies and practices that will propel you towards financial greatness.

But remember, this is not the end—it is only the beginning.

Financial greatness is not merely an achievement but a lifelong pursuit. It requires ongoing commitment, continuous learning, and a dedication to personal and professional growth. It demands resilience in the face of challenges, adaptability to evolving circumstances, and a mindset of abundance and generosity.

As you move forward on your path to financial greatness, hold steadfast to your goals, dreams, and values. Embrace the opportunities that come your way, and never shy away from calculated risks. Surround yourself with like-minded individuals who support and inspire you. Continuously seek knowledge, refine your skills, and adapt to the changing tides of the financial world.

But amidst all the ambition and pursuit of wealth, remember to find joy and fulfillment along the way. Pause to appreciate your progress, celebrate your achievements, and nourish your relationships. Give back to others and make a positive impact in the lives of those around you.

Your path to financial greatness is unique, and it will unfold in its own time and in its own way. Embrace the journey with enthusiasm, curiosity, and a hunger for personal growth. Stay true to yourself, trust in your abilities, and never lose sight of the impact you can make in the world.

Now, it is time to take what you have learned, put it into action, and embark on your own remarkable path to financial greatness. The possibilities are boundless, and the future is yours to shape. Believe in yourself, embrace the journey, and let your dreams soar.

Wishing you all the success, fulfillment, and financial greatness that you deserve.

Appendix: Resources and Tools for Continued Growth

In this appendix, you will find a curated list of resources and tools that will support your continued growth and development on your path to financial greatness. These resources encompass various aspects of wealth building, personal development, and financial education. They are designed to provide you with valuable information, practical tools, and additional guidance as you navigate your journey towards financial success.

Books:
"Rich Dad Poor Dad" by Robert Kiyosaki
"Think and Grow Rich" by Napoleon Hill
"The Millionaire Next Door" by Thomas J. Stanley and William D. Danko
"The Intelligent Investor" by Benjamin Graham
"The 4-Hour Workweek" by Timothy Ferriss

Online Courses and Programs:
Financial Literacy courses on platforms like Coursera, Udemy, and Khan Academy
Wealth and Success mindset programs by renowned coaches and experts
Entrepreneurship and business development courses

Podcasts:
"The Dave Ramsey Show" hosted by Dave Ramsey
"The Smart Passive Income Online Business and Blogging Podcast" hosted by Pat Flynn
"The Tim Ferriss Show" hosted by Tim Ferriss
"The Tony Robbins Podcast" hosted by Tony Robbins

Financial Planning Tools:
Personal finance apps for budgeting, expense tracking, and goal setting
Investment tracking platforms for monitoring your portfolio performance
Retirement planning calculators and tools

Professional Associations and Communities:
Join local networking groups and business associations
Online communities and forums dedicated to entrepreneurship, investing, and personal finance
Attend conferences, seminars, and workshops related to wealth building and financial education

Mentorship and Coaching:
Seek out mentors who have achieved the level of success you aspire to
Engage with professional coaches or join mastermind groups for ongoing guidance and support

Financial News and Publications:
Stay updated with financial news through reputable sources like The Wall Street Journal, Forbes, Bloomberg, and Financial Times
Subscribe to industry-specific newsletters and magazines for insights and trends

Charitable Organizations and Volunteering Opportunities:
Identify reputable charities aligned with causes you care about and explore ways to contribute
Get involved in volunteering activities to give back to your community and make a positive impact

Remember, these resources are meant to complement and enhance your journey towards financial greatness. Continuously seek knowledge, stay informed, and be open to learning from various sources. Tailor your selections based on your specific goals and interests, and adapt as your needs evolve.

May these resources serve as valuable tools in your pursuit of financial greatness and personal fulfillment. Embrace the opportunity to learn, grow, and make a positive impact on your own life and the lives of others.

Note: The mentioned resources are suggestions and should be evaluated based on their relevance and applicability to your specific circumstances and preferences.

Disclaimer

"The Millionaire Mindset Blueprint: Unleash Your Potential and Build Wealth" is intended for general educational and informational purposes only. The author and publisher of this book are not financial advisors or professionals, and the content should not be considered as personalized financial advice.

The information provided in this book is based on the author's personal experiences, research, and understanding of wealth creation. While every effort has been made to ensure the accuracy and reliability of the information presented, financial landscapes and individual circumstances can vary significantly. Therefore, it is recommended that readers consult with a qualified financial advisor or professional before making any financial decisions or implementing strategies discussed in this book.

The author does not guarantee the success or outcomes of applying the principles, strategies, or techniques outlined in this book. Individual results may vary, and financial success depends on a variety of factors, including but not limited to personal dedication, market conditions, and economic factors.

Readers are encouraged to conduct their own due diligence, research, and analysis before making any financial decisions. The author and publisher disclaim any liability for any loss or damage incurred directly or indirectly from the use or application of the information presented in this book.

By reading this book, readers acknowledge and agree that they are solely responsible for their own financial decisions and outcomes. They should use their judgment and consult with professionals when necessary to ensure the suitability and appropriateness of any financial strategies or actions taken.

Please note that laws, regulations, and financial practices may vary across countries and jurisdictions. Readers are advised to consider local laws and regulations before applying any financial strategies or concepts discussed in this book.

Remember, financial success requires ongoing learning, adaptability, and diligent effort. The author and publisher are not responsible for any decisions or actions taken based on the information presented in this book.

Made in the USA
Middletown, DE
12 November 2024

64375856R00049